Books are to be returned o...

THE
COMPLETE BOOK
OF THE SEASONS

Sally Tagholm

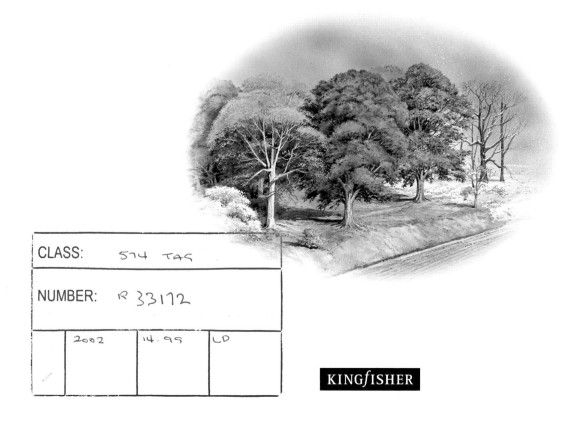

KINGFISHER

Managing Editor   Melissa Fairley
Editor   Hannah Wilson
Designer   Jane Buckley
Production   Debbie Otter
DTP manager   Nicky Studdart
Picture research manager   Jane Lambert
Picture research   Rachael Swann
Artwork archivists   Wendy Allison and Steve Robinson

The publisher would like to thank the following illustrators:
Susanna Addario, Mike Atkinson, Andrea Brun, John Butler,
Peter Dennis (Linda Rogers Associates), Ray Grinaway, Ian Jackson (Wildlife Art),
Kevin Madison, Sebastian Quidley, Mike Saunders, Roger Stewart (Kevin Jones Associates),
Richard Ward, Gareth Williams and Dan Wright

The publisher would also like to thank the following for supplying photographs:
Corbis: 12tl, 24bl; Ardea London: 26tl; NHPA: 26cl; Corbis: 30bl; Science Photo Library,
Tom McHugh: 45br; Frank Lane Picture Agency, David Hosking: 46c;
www.osf.uk.com, Scott Winer: 49bl; Popperfoto, David Joiner: 50tl;
Eye Ubiquitous, ©John Dakers: 52bl; Still Pictures, Julio Etchart: 66bl;
Still Pictures, Ron Giling: 84bl; Popperfoto: 90bl; P. A. Photos: 93cr
Every effort has been made to trace the copyright holders of the photographs.
The publisher apologizes for any inconvenience caused.

KINGFISHER

Kingfisher Publications Plc
New Penderel House, 283–288 High Holborn
London WC1V 7HZ
www.kingfisherpub.com

First published by Kingfisher Publications Plc in 2002
2 4 6 8 10 9 7 5 3 1

1TR/0502/TWP/CLSN(CLSN)/150ENSOMA

Copyright © Kingfisher Publications Plc 2002

ISBN 0 7534 0696 9

Printed in Singapore

CONTENTS

THE SEASONS 4

CHANGING SEASONS 6
The four seasons 8
Hot and cold 10
Wet and dry 12
Wind and waves 14

SPRING 16
Spring showers 18
Spring flowers 20
Pond life 22
Spring farming 24
Spring cleaning 26
In the park 28
Spring nights 30
St Patrick's Day 32
Bun Bang Fai 34

SUMMER 36
Summer sun 38
Keeping cool 40
Summer insects 42
Summertime 44
Summer farming 46
Summer holiday 48
Summer sports 50

Midnight sun festival 52
Verona opera festival 54

AUTUMN 56
Autumn winds 58
Autumn colours 60
Autumn fauna 62
Autumn farming 64
Autumn and us 66
Up in the air 68
Thanksgiving 70
Chinese moon festival 72

WINTER 74
Winter chills 76
Hibernation 78
Migration 80
Wintertime 82
Winter farming 84
Winter playtime 86
Winter sports 88
Sapporo's snow festival 90
New Year 92

CALENDAR 94

INDEX 96

THE SEASONS

As the year goes by, neatly divided into months and weeks and days, the seasons unfold and change, transforming the world around us and the things we do. Spring, summer, autumn and winter sometimes creep up slowly, one sliding seamlessly into the next, but at other times, they arrive unannounced, a sudden dramatic change, impossible to miss.

CHANGING SEASONS

In most countries, there are four seasons every year – spring, summer, autumn and winter. Each one lasts for about three months and has its own particular kind of weather and temperature. The hours of daylight also vary enormously, according to the season. On a cold, dark winter's evening, it is hard to remember the long, hot days of summer – let alone splashing in the sea or lying in the sun.

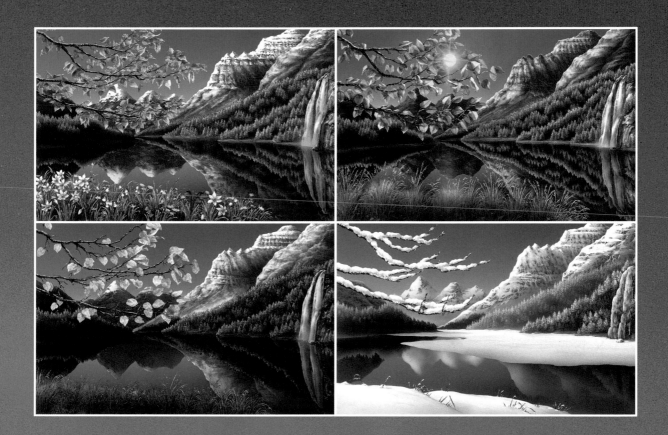

The four seasons

From the beginning of time, people have recognized the importance of the seasons and celebrated them in many different ways. No matter where you live, what language you speak or which calendar you use, the seasons follow their own rhythm in a never-ending cycle. It is the same pattern, year after year. Each season is quite different from the next, and just as important, changing the natural world around us in its own unique way.

Spring announces birth and renewal while the summer brings sun and warmth to make everything grow and ripen. In autumn, nature begins to slow down, ready for its long winter sleep. We, also, change with the seasons – our energies waxing and waning with the sun. In the short, dark days of winter, we curl up and keep warm at home, like seeds under the bleak, bare earth. As soon as spring arrives, we open doors and windows and want to be outside, enjoying the fresh air. In summer, we soak up the sun, like the sunflowers in the fields, and in autumn we get out our gloves and scarves, knowing that winter will soon be here again.

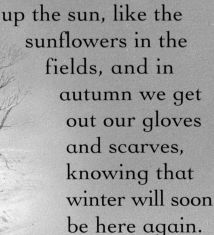

Other planets in the solar system
have seasons too. These are caused
by the way the planets tilt or by their
varying distance from the sun as they orbit
it in huge uneven loops. Mars has four seasons,
just like earth, but because a Martian year is as long
as two years on earth, its seasons are also much longer.
Mercury, on the other hand, has no atmosphere, so there
is no wind or rain, and no protection against the sun's heat.
With days and nights each lasting about three earth months, and
with the planet swinging closer and farther from the sun, temperatures
can range from 420°C to -180°C. The planet Uranus has very unusual
seasons. The south pole has a summer lasting 42 years, when the sun
never sets, while the opposite pole is plunged into darkness for 42 years.

In recent years, many of the world's leading scientists have warned
that the earth is warming up because of pollution from burning fossil
fuels. It is thought that global warming is causing weather patterns
to change, as the ice caps melt and the sea levels rise. It is also quite
possible that it is making the seasons shift slightly, with earlier
springs, longer summers and milder winters.

Each year, the seasons change because of the way the earth spins round on its own axis as it orbits the sun. It rotates tilted to one side, at an angle of 23.5° from the vertical. This means that first one half of the globe, and then the other, leans towards the sun. In December, when the North Pole tilts away from the sun, countries in the northern hemisphere have winter. At the same time, the South Pole is tilted towards the sun so countries in the southern hemisphere are having their summer. In June, the opposite happens to both hemispheres as earth's tilt changes.

Hot and cold

In some countries near the equator, it is hot all the year round and the sun is always high overhead. In the polar regions, the temperature rarely rises above freezing point.

In Antarctica the sun disappears completely during the winter and temperatures can drop to -50°C. The size of the continent almost doubles as the pack ice surrounding it freezes.

Most deserts are hot all the year round and rain is very rare indeed. There are no clouds to block the sun and the temperatures are extreme. Lack of water is a problem for animals and plants alike but they have evolved and adapted to cope with the conditions. The Bactrian, or Asian, camel can survive for long periods (5 to 7 days) without food or water because it stores fats and oils in its two humps to give it energy.

The adult male penguins huddle together to conserve heat, taking it in turns to stand on the outside where freezing winds sweep past.

But the flightless birds which live there are well adapted to the bitter cold, insulated with layers of fat, thick skin and dense feathers which trap warm air. Emperor penguins live in colonies near the sea and breed during the harsh winter. The female lays a single egg and disappears to feed, leaving the male to incubate the egg by himself. For nine weeks he balances the egg on his feet where it is protected by his soft warm body. By the time the female returns, the male will have lost up to a third of his bodyweight. She now feeds the newly hatched chick while her partner sets off for the sea.

11

Wet and dry

Some regions a few degrees north and south of the equator, such as parts of South America and Africa, are hot and dry for most of the year. They have one, or sometimes two, rainy seasons each year.

In southern Asia, the summer monsoon season lasts from June to September each year. The torrential rains blow in from the ocean as the direction of the wind changes to come from the south west. The southern tip of India is the first to feel the long awaited rains – its arrival is vital for next year's crops. But, if the rains are even heavier than usual, they can cause terrible flooding. In 1988, 28 million people lost their homes in Bangladesh.

The grasslands – or savannas – of Africa, South America and northern Australia all suffer during the long, hot dry season. During this time, the landscape is parched by the sun – the grass shrivels and turns yellow, the trees lose their leaves. Trees such as acacia and baobab survive because they have very long roots that tap groundwater from deep below the surface. The baobab also has a huge fireproof trunk which stores water like a sponge. The bushmen of the Kalahari use hollow grasses, like straws, to drink the precious water from deep inside.

In order to survive, herds of grazing animals, such as zebra and elephants, have to travel huge distances over the plains looking for water. Smaller creatures, such as meerkats and ground squirrels, burrow under the ground to escape the heat and avoid losing too much moisture.

Wind and waves

Late spring and early summer is the tornado – or 'twister' – season in the Great Plains of the United States. Tornadoes also occur in Australia, Canada, the United Kingdom, Italy, Japan and Central Asia.

Tornadoes can form suddenly when warm, moist air cools and rises to form great towering thunderclouds. Cold air rushes in to replace the rising air, creating strong winds. If this starts to rotate faster and faster, a funnel-shaped tornado is formed, stretching down from the thundercloud.

Tornadoes get their name from the Latin word for twist or turn. To begin with, they are made up of millions of tiny water droplets – just like any cloud. But as soon as they touch the ground, they start to suck up earth and dirt, and turn almost black. They can pick up anything in their path – houses, cars, buses and animals – and the wind speeds inside the tornado can reach 800 kilometres per hour.

Tropical revolving storms called hurricanes occur in the Atlantic from 1 June to 30 November. They form over the ocean when warm air rises so fast that it creates a region of intense low pressure beneath it. More and more air is pulled in creating a huge spiralling weather system. When the wind speed reaches 120 kilometres per hour, it becomes a hurricane.

Hurricanes can be 400 kilometres wide, with winds spiralling furiously inside. To the north of the equator they blow in an anti-clockwise direction, to the south of the equator they blow in a clockwise direction. At the very centre, or eye of the storm, everything is still and calm and the temperatures are very high. Similar storms are known as typhoons in the Pacific Ocean and cyclones in the Indian Ocean.

A huge storm often accompanies a hurricane, cyclone or typhoon as it races across the ocean towards land. The waters are sucked up by the low pressure, forming a gigantic wall of water. Some waves reach a height of 30 metres and cause severe flooding in low-lying coastal areas, such as Bangladesh, Pakistan and northwest India. In February 1953, a massive storm surge flooded areas of the Netherlands, killing 2,000 people. In 1969, Hurricane Camille (hurricanes are usually given names, alternately male and female) devastated the coasts of Florida and Mississippi, and an 8.2 metre storm surge drowned 300 people. Meteorologists are constantly working out better ways of predicting hurricanes to try to save lives.

SPRING

Spring brings new life to the world, after the quiet cold months of winter. The weather begins to get warmer and the days longer. Bright flowers appear, creatures emerge from their winter hibernation and birds start singing in the early morning air. Farmers are busy in their fields, planting new crops and tending the new-born lambs.

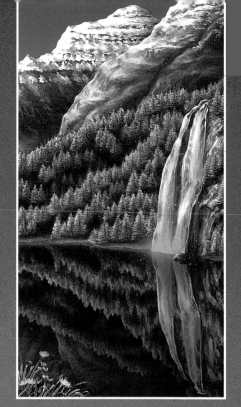

Spring showers

As spring arrives the days get longer and the earth begins to warm up after the long winter months. But the weather can change very quickly, with bright sunshine one moment and rain the next.

Spring is famous for its sudden showers and downpours that water the land and encourage everything to grow. It is also the time of year when the sun starts to get stronger and climbs a little higher in the sky. Brand new buds begin to appear on the trees and the first spring flowers come out.

Different kinds of cloud bring changes to the weather. The huge white clouds that are known as 'cumulonimbus' (left) get their name from the Latin words for 'puffy' and 'rain-bearing'. They often tower high in the sky in great thunder shower formations that look like giant anvils. Like all clouds, they are formed when the water vapour rises, then cools and condenses into millions of tiny droplets of water. These clouds get larger and larger as they collect more and more moisture and then fall to earth as rain.

Because of the changeable weather, spring is one of the best times of the year to see rainbows. They appear suddenly when the sun comes out from behind a cloud but it is still raining. The colours of the rainbow are always in the same order – with red at the top, followed by orange, yellow, green, blue, indigo and violet.

Spring is a good time for putting on your raincoat and boots and splashing about in puddles. The first waterproof boot was invented in 1815 and named after the Duke of Wellington.

A raindrop acts like a prism, bending and refracting the rays of the sun to form a rainbow. It breaks the sunlight up into the seven colours of the rainbow, which is called the spectrum.

A thermometer measures how hot or cold the air is. Thermometers contain some mercury or alcohol, which moves up a narrow tube when it gets hot and falls back again when it is cold.

19

Spring flowers

After the bleak, bare days of winter, tender new shoots push through the earth as spring arrives. Tight buds uncurl and open, as if by magic, turning into bright spring flowers, and opening their faces to the sun.

In early spring, the tiny pink flowers of the spring beauty creep across woods and stream banks like a starry carpet. They open only when the sun is shining. Spring beauty is sometimes known as 'fairy spuds' because it grows from a small tuber that looks like a little potato.

Dangling catkins (male), or lambs' tails, open very early in spring, before leaves appear on the hazel tree. They have been developing since the autumn and each one has more than 100 tiny flowers on it. The catkins release their yellow pollen as they swing in the wind.

Many of the flowers that bloom in spring – such as crocus, daffodil, hyacinth and tulip – grow from round bulbs or knobbly corms. They are planted in autumn and spend the winter buried safely underground, waiting for the first hint of warm weather before they start sprouting.

All sorts of bulbs are cultivated in different countries around the world but Holland is particularly famous for its bulb farms. In spring, huge fields of flowers stretch as far as the eye can see, like great splashes of colour in a giant paint box. But long ago, in the 17th century, some bulbs were so rare and valuable that single specimens changed hands for incredible sums of money. One tulip bulb, known as a 'Semper Augustus', was sold for 3,000 Dutch guilders – the equivalent of £1,050.

Daffodils are perhaps the best-loved of all spring flowers with their long green stems and friendly, nodding faces. Strangely enough, the bulb and leaves contain poisonous crystals, which means they are eaten by only a handful of insects.

Pond life

For most of the year, a pond is a peaceful place with only the odd duck or moorhen to be seen. In springtime, however, it becomes a hive of activity, as creatures both above and below the surface of the water prepare for the breeding season.

Dragonfly nymphs change their skins as they grow and, after the fifth or sixth change, their wings begin to form. They climb out of the water, clinging tightly to the weeds, and shed their skins for the last time, emerging as beautiful dragonflies.

Pond plants, such as water irises, often grow along the water's edge. Water irises, sometimes called yellow flags, bring a vivid splash of colour to ponds in springtime. Water lilies, on the other hand, anchor their long roots in mud at the pond's bottom, while their broad leaves float on the water's surface.

The great diving beetle likes to eat tadpoles, pond snails and small fish. In spring, the female lays her eggs inside the stems of water plants. When the larva hatches, it looks like a strange, pale, shrimp-like insect. It clings to plants and weeds so that it does not float to the surface.

In the breeding season the male smooth newt is brightly coloured and has a wavy crest along his back. He often performs a special courtship dance, arching his back and flicking his tail, to impress the female. She lays her eggs one at a time in a nice, safe place – under a leaf or a waterweed.

22

In spring, male woodpeckers mark out their territory and attract females by drumming sharply on the bark of a tree with their beaks. It is rather like a secret code – each bird pecking out his message to a slightly different rhythm, letting everybody know that he is there. The males usually stop doing this when they begin nesting.

Moorhens usually build their nests out of old, dried water plants and reeds near the water's edge. Sometimes they use old nests abandoned by other birds in bushes nearby. The female lays a clutch of between 5 and 11 eggs, which is incubated by both parents.

Soon after baby ducks hatch out of their eggs, they follow their mother to the pond, splashing happily into the water. They can swim immediately and, before long, learn to find food for themselves. When these young mallards are fully grown, the male will be more colourful than the female.

Each spring, when it is the breeding season, frogs come back to the pond to mate. The females lay their eggs in clumps of clear jelly, which float just below the surface of the water. These are known as frogspawn. The tiny tadpoles which hatch from the eggs gradually grow legs, turning into small froglets after about 12 or 13 weeks.

23

Spring farming

The farming year has followed the cycle of the seasons since people first started to cultivate the land. Each year follows the same familiar pattern, which shapes farmers' lives all over the world.

Spring is one of the busiest times of the year with many different jobs to be done on the farm. As soon as the last chills of winter disappear, the fields are prepared and planted with seeds for summer crops, and cattle are led out from their sheds to new pasture.

Lambing, which usually starts in late winter, goes on throughout early spring. The grass is lush and green after all the rain, and the ewes (female sheep) produce rich and nourishing milk which helps their wobbling lambs to grow. Soon the lambs are strong enough to race around the field and gambol in the spring sunshine. They are weaned from their mothers by the time they are six months old.

Rice is the staple food of more than half the people in the world and needs a warm climate and lots of water to grow. At first, the crop is planted in dry fields but, as soon as it starts to sprout, the seedlings are transplanted by hand to rice paddies. These are pools of water that have been dug out and prepared, with a small wall of earth around each one. Sometimes, to make sure that the bottom of the paddy is soft enough for the roots of seedlings, the farmer drives his cattle round and round to break up the earth. The seedlings are carefully planted out, one at a time, under the water in neat, straight lines. Later on in the year, when the rice is ripe, the paddies are drained before harvesting.

Spring cleaning

Spring is traditionally the season of rebirth and renewal when the whole world seems to wake up after the long cold months of winter. Everything is filled with new energy – including us!

The bright spring sunshine that floods in through the windows shows up all the dust and dirt of winter. So it is not surprising that many people give their home a good clean.

Nowadays, we have all sorts of machines and gadgets to help us clean the house. Soon we might even have robots to sweep the floor or polish the table for us. But long ago, when everything had to be done by hand, spring cleaning the house could take days or even weeks. Open fires that smoked and blazed all winter, producing lots of ash and soot, used to make everything very dirty.

Traditionally, spring cleaning used to start around the time of the vernal – or spring – equinox, when days and nights are the same length. This is also the first day of spring – 20 or 21 March in the northern hemisphere and 22 or 23 September in the southern hemisphere. From this time, the days will be getting much longer and warmer, so you can put away your winter clothes and begin to think about the summer ahead. It is time to tidy up – perhaps even to find lost treasures that disappeared many months ago.

Boatyards, marinas and harbours hum with activity in spring and the smell of paint and varnish fills the air. It is the time of year when boats are repainted and repaired to ensure they're seaworthy.

The first successful vacuum cleaner, invented in 1901, was the size of a milk float and was manned by four to six people. The first upright vacuum cleaner (for use by one person) was developed in 1907.

Eostre was the ancient goddess of spring in northern Europe and was often pictured with a basket of eggs and a hare or rabbit. She represented the rebirth of the earth and of all growing things.

27

In the park

As spring arrives and the days get longer, bright sunshine casts its spell over the world again. It lures people out into the fresh, mild air – thick, winter clothes can be put away and forgotten for another year.

The park, which has been still and bare for most of the winter, is beginning to stir. Some of the trees are dotted with tiny green buds and the early pink blossom has suddenly appeared. The birds are building their nests, ready to lay their eggs, and ducks are hungry, waiting to be fed.

On bright spring days, there are lots of people in the park, enjoying the sun – and the smell of newly mown grass, which fills the air for the first time since last summer. The park keepers have been busy getting everything ready for another year – painting and mending. Dogs bark and race around, chasing their tails, and fetching sticks and balls. Children play on the swings, swoop down the slides and ride their bikes.

There are special skateparks where skateboarders can enjoy themselves. There is usually a large concrete 'half pipe' in the middle of the park, which looks like a gigantic letter 'U'. Skaters practise their most daring tricks on it, speeding up and down the smooth curves at great speed, flying through the air. They always wear helmets, and pads to protect their knees and elbows, and baggy clothes so they can move about comfortably, and safely. There are all sorts of different tricks but one of the most popular is an 'air' when all four wheels of the skateboard leave the ground at the same time.

Some trees
come into leaf
and are covered
with a haze of green,
while the branches of
others are still quite bare.
The silver birch and the willow
are two of the first to show
their new spring leaves.

In some parks, dogs
can play anywhere,
but in others they
have to be kept on
leads. Owners clear up
any dog mess and put
it in special waste bins.

Spring nights

Warm spring nights are perfect for star-gazing – especially if you have got a pair of binoculars or a telescope. You can explore the universe from your own back garden.

Each spring, new constellations – or patterns of stars – appear in the night sky, marking the passing of the seasons. In the northern hemisphere, Orion and its neighbouring constellations slowly drift out of sight and others come into view.

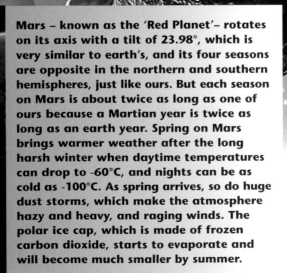

Mars – known as the 'Red Planet'– rotates on its axis with a tilt of 23.98°, which is very similar to earth's, and its four seasons are opposite in the northern and southern hemispheres, just like ours. But each season on Mars is about twice as long as one of ours because a Martian year is twice as long as an earth year. Spring on Mars brings warmer weather after the long harsh winter when daytime temperatures can drop to -60°C, and nights can be as cold as -100°C. As spring arrives, so do huge dust storms, which make the atmosphere hazy and heavy, and raging winds. The polar ice cap, which is made of frozen carbon dioxide, starts to evaporate and will become much smaller by summer.

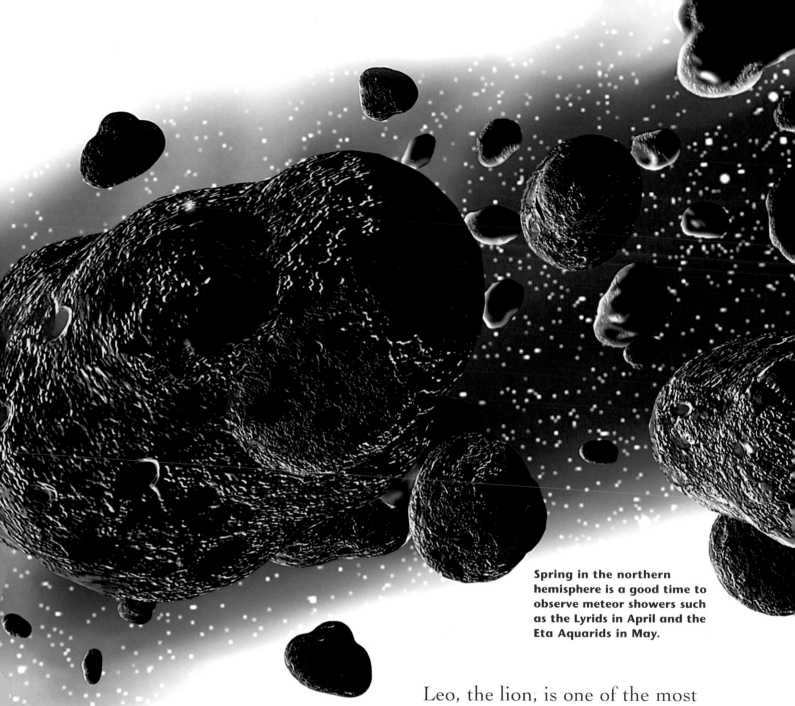

Leo, the lion, is one of the most spectacular constellations of all. His head and front paws look like a backwards question mark made out of stars. This is often known as the Sickle. At the bottom of it there is a brilliant star called Regulus, which means 'little king'. It is approximately 85 light years away and shines 160 times brighter than our sun – it also has a bluish-white tinge.

On clear, moonless nights, you might see some meteors streaking across the sky. Meteor showers are caused when earth passes through a cloud of space debris left by a passing comet.

31

St Patrick's Day

The feast of St Patrick, the patron saint of Ireland, is a national holiday on 17 March. It is celebrated by Irish people all round the world. For example, in the United States, millions of Irish-Americans hold huge street parades in more than 100 cities.

St Patrick lived more than 1,500 years ago and is generally thought to have brought Christianity to Ireland. He was, in fact, born in Wales in AD 385 but spent 30 years of his life travelling around Ireland setting up monasteries, churches and schools. It is said that he gave a sermon from a hilltop that drove all the snakes from Ireland. Some people think this was another way of saying he converted the pagans to Christianity.

There is a carnival atmosphere on St Patrick's Day – and everyone enjoys the decorated floats, marching bands and traditional Irish dancers. People join the parade dressed in green, their faces and hair also painted green. Or they take part in fancy dress – often as leprechauns, the little shoemakers from Irish folk tales. Everyone wears a shamrock, the three-leafed clover associated with St Patrick.

The first public St Patrick's Day celebrations in the United States were held in Boston in 1737. The first American St Patrick's Day Parade took place when Irish soldiers serving in the English army marched through New York City in 1762.

The beginning of spring is celebrated by the Hindu festival of Holi in India. It can last for two or three days. On the night of the full moon, during the spring harvest, a large bonfire is lit and the direction of the flames is thought to show which land will be especially fertile in the coming year. Garlands of cow dung (cows are sacred in India) are thrown in the fire. Offerings of wheat and grain are made, and coconuts, symbols of new life, are roasted in the fire. It is also a festival of colour, symbolizing fertility. People cover each other in coloured paints (gulal).

Bun Bang Fai

Each year, in the second week of May, a rocket festival known as Bun Bang Fai is held in north-eastern Thailand. It is the end of the long dry season and traditionally the time of year when farmers pray for rain for their crops.

According to legend, there was once a rain god called Vassakan who loved being worshipped by fire. A rocket – or 'Bang Fai' – was made by local people and sent high in the sky to where the rain god lived. The people hoped that Vassakan would respond and bless them with rain.

The two-day festival has been celebrated for centuries, and nowadays people come from all over the world to watch the dazzling displays. On the first day of the festival, there are parades and on the second day, the rockets are launched.

It is believed that if the rockets shoot high in the air the village will be blessed with rain and there will be plenty of food in the coming season. Before the launching ceremony, Buddhist monks bless the rockets.

Toonik Tyme celebrates the coming of spring in Nunavut, a Canadian territory in the eastern Arctic. The traditional Inuit festivities include igloo-building competitions and a special appearance by the 'Tuniq' who is a bit like an Arctic Easter bunny, but dressed in caribou skins. Inuit games are played, there are snowmobile runs and dog-team racing. The Canadian Inuit dogs, known as 'Qimmiq' in Inuktitut, are perfectly adapted to the Arctic climate and live on a diet of meat and fat. These dogs have lived in the Arctic for over 4,000 years.

The rockets are all home-made, constructed out of bamboo, or wooden tubes, with colourful designs painted on them. Competitions are held for the biggest rocket or for the one that can fly the highest. Some of the rockets are huge – up to nine metres long – and packed with up to 25 kilograms of gunpowder.

SUMMER

The sun is high overhead and at its strongest during the long, hot days of summer. Flowers and fields are in full bloom and bees are busy collecting pollen and nectar. Crops ripen slowly in the warmth and summer fruits are ready to pick. The beach is crowded with holidaymakers, enjoying the sunshine.

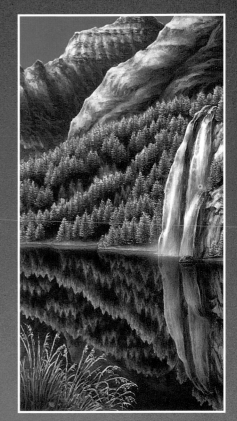

Activity on the surface of the sun, such as sunspots, flares and solar storms, follows an 11 year cycle. At its peak, the wind can rise to gale force and the ensuing effects can be felt all over earth.

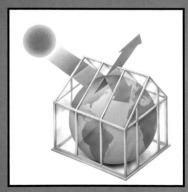

The Campbell Stokes Sunshine Recorder counts the daily hours of sunshine. A glass ball focuses the sun's rays onto a piece of card, burning a horizontal line (or dots if the sun moves in or out of the clouds).

Many leading scientists now believe that the earth is warming up because of the 'greenhouse effect'. This means that some gases, such as carbon dioxide, trap energy from the sun and do not allow heat to escape back into space.

Summer Sun

The sun is our nearest star and the source of all light, warmth and life on earth. Its yearly journey marks the passing of the seasons. In summer, it travels much higher each day and its rays are stronger, encouraging everything to grow.

The sun has been burning for about five billion years. The temperature at its core is 15 million°C and its light travels at about 300,000 kilometres per second. This means that it takes approximately eight-and-a-half minutes for sunlight to reach us.

Because the earth rotates at an angle and is tilted to one side, the sun appears directly overhead at different latitudes during the year. In the northern hemisphere, the summer solstice (21 or 22 June) is the time when the sun reaches its most northerly point, over the Tropic of Cancer (23°, 27 minutes north). The longest day of the year, with the most hours of sunlight, falls at this time – it is generally known as the beginning of summer. It has always been an important time of year, celebrated by different religions and cultures around the world. The word 'solstice' comes from the Latin word 'solstitium' which means 'sun standing still'. This is just what the sun appears to do – changing its angle extremely slowly from day to day.

It is not the hottest part of the summer – it usually takes another few weeks for earth to warm up. In the southern hemisphere, the opposite is happening at the same time, and it is the winter solstice and the shortest day.

Although the summer is usually the hottest time of the year, earth is in fact furthest away from the sun at this time of year. This is because it does not travel around the sun in an exact circle but in an oval loop. In July, we are 155 million kilometres away from the sun whereas in January, we are 150 million kilometres from it.

> **WARNING:** You should never look at the sun directly and certainly never through a telescope or binoculars – you could be blinded for life.

Keeping cool

Many creatures have evolved so that they can cool down automatically when the weather gets very hot. Others have to change their behaviour to keep out of the sun and avoid the baking heat.

Most mammals have special sweat glands which start working when it gets hot. The glands cover the skin with moisture which then evaporates, cooling the body down.

Some mammals, like rodents and opossums, have a different technique altogether. They produce saliva in their mouths and then lick it all over their fur. Many other creatures cool down by splashing in a pond or river.

The crocodile, a cold-blooded creature, soaks up warmth from the sun and then lies with its mouth wide open. The skin inside the mouth is very thin with lots of blood vessels near the surface. As air circulates, moisture evaporates from the mouth.

The horse needs shade and lots of water to drink when temperatures are very high. It sweats all over its body to try to keep itself cool. The sweat contains a protein which forms a lather – like whipped egg whites – when the horse is extremely hot.

The camel can survive extreme heat and last for almost a week without water. The long hair on its head, throat, neck and hump help protect it from sunburn. Another mammal which is physically adapted for extreme heat is the tiny fennec fox. Its enormous ears act as conductors to help get rid of the heat. Some snakes and lizards keep cool by opening their mouths and gaping widely. The desert iguana even pants like a dog with its tongue hanging out.

The dog does not have any sweat glands – except on the pads of the feet. It lowers its body temperature by opening its mouth and panting, which allows moisture to evaporate from its lungs, cooling it down.

To keep cool, the elephant sprays water over itself with its trunk, rolls in cool, wet mud and flaps its ears to lower the temperature of blood as it circulates round the body.

41

Summer insects

The long, hot days of summer are full of the sounds of insects, buzzing and swarming and scuttling. They are out and about in their hordes, feeding on newly grown plants. Some eat the leaves, roots, seeds and sap, others prefer the nectar and pollen, hidden inside the flowers.

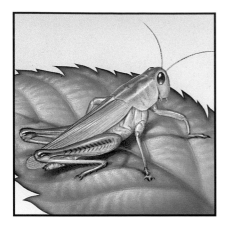

Male grasshoppers and crickets sing in the summer by rubbing together two parts of their body. They do this to attract females. Grasshoppers rub their legs, which have a row of tiny pegs on them, against their front wings. Each kind of grasshopper makes a different sound. Crickets rub an upturned scraper on one forewing along a row of 50 to 250 teeth on the underside of the other wing.

There are about 1,900 species of fireflies – or lightning bugs – that twinkle and shine on summer nights. They have light organs on the undersides of their bodies, and the males flash special patterns of light to attract females. The females signal in response – the rhythm and sequence of the light is like a secret code. Some species of firefly have luminescent larvae called glow worms.

Honey bees are very busy in summer when there are plenty of flowers in full bloom, sometimes flying as far as five kilometres to find a good source of nectar. Their favourite flowers are usually blue or purple, followed by yellow or orange. They gather nectar from deep inside the flowers, sucking it up with their long tongues. At the same time, they pick up a dusting of pollen on their hind legs. They then fly back to the hive with their precious trophies, which will be used as food for the entire bee colony. The pollen provides protein and the nectar is converted into honey, which provides carbohydrate.

The colony is a carefully organized community with a queen, up to 500 drones (males) and 60,000 workers (females), all of which have their allotted tasks. When a scout bee has found a good new source of nectar, she communicates this to the other workers by flying in circles and wagging her tail.

Summertime

We all look forward to the summer and being outside, enjoying the sunshine. But the sun can be extremely hot at this time of year, and its rays intense. This heat can affect our bodies in different ways.

During summer, it is important to keep out of the sun when it is high in the sky. In some countries, people take a siesta, or nap, at midday when it is hottest.

Your body has its own built-in thermostat – the hypothalamus, the brain's 'master gland', which helps the body maintain a constant temperature. During hot weather, this gland detects a rise in blood temperature, and sends out a signal that causes the blood to flow more rapidly and closer to the surface of the skin, cooling it. The hypothalamus can also call another natural cooling system into play – sweat. The evaporation of moisture from our skin when we sweat, cools our body.

But your body needs extra help in summer. Drink lots of fluids regularly to avoid becoming dehydrated and wear a hat to protect your head. Sun hats come in all sorts of shapes and sizes and can be made of cotton, canvas or coconut leaves!

Use suntan lotion to protect your skin from the sun's harmful ultraviolet, or UV, rays. It's not just people who need this sort of protection – farmers often rub sun cream on their pigs in summertime! Wear white loose-fitting clothing in summer. White reflects heat and loose clothes allow air to circulate, keeping your body cool.

It's not all bad news – the sun is our main source of vitamin D, which helps the body to absorb bone-strengthening calcium and phosphorus. And sunlight stimulates hormones that make us feel happy!

Sundials tell us the time on sunny days. The upright part, the 'gnomon', casts its shadow onto the hourly markings as the earth turns during the day.

In ancient Egypt, where the sun god Re was worshipped, the pharaoh Tutankhamun was kept cool by ostrich-feather fans on long, gold poles.

Before fridges and freezers arrived in the 1920s, blocks of ice were delivered several times a week and stored in wooden cupboards called iceboxes.

Long, sun-filled summer days are perfect for generating electricity from solar panels. Houses and even cars can be powered by the sun.

45

Summer farming

In summer, the sun is at its strongest and the fields are full of all sorts of different crops, such as corn and sunflowers. The farmers make hay from the long, sweet grass, while the weather is hot and dry.

Sunflowers are now grown commercially all over the world and are an important crop both for their oil and for their seeds. They were originally native to North America and were used by native Americans for food and for oil.

After they are planted in late spring or early summer, sunflowers grow quickly and flower, painting the fields a bright yellow. Their roots go deep and spread out wide so they are able to find water and survive a certain amount of drought. At first, their heads face east in morning and west in evening, following the sun on its journey through the sky each day. Once the flowers have fully opened, they usually face east. This is when the seeds are fully exposed and the large flower heads act as perfect feeding perches for passing hungry birds.

Strawberries need the right weather conditions and can be ruined by a late frost, too much rain and not enough sun. They can also be spoiled by too much sun and not enough rain. After the flowers bloom on the strawberry plant, it takes about a month for the fruit to ripen. In June, when the harvest starts, there are strawberries in all sorts of different stages of development on the plants – tiny green berries, big white berries and ripe red berries. Each plant is picked two or three times a week – unlike other types of fruit, once the berries have been picked, they do not ripen any further. They are picked, sorted and packed by hand, and then exported worldwide. Some native Americans still celebrate strawberry Thanksgiving during mid- to late-June.

Summer holiday

On a hot summer's day, the beach is a perfect playground – as long as you've got your swimming costume, a bucket and spade, and a beach ball. And it is a treasure trove, too, where you never know what you will find hidden beneath the sand.

The tide sweeps in and out, constantly cleaning the sand, making it shiny and new – damp sand is perfect for digging and building sandcastles.

As the water retreats, it leaves all sorts of interesting things behind it – including driftwood, which has been shaped by the pounding of the waves, smooth stones, fish skeletons and seaweed. Usually there are thousands of shells, too, in a dazzling array of shapes and sizes. They are the empty homes of small soft creatures known as molluscs. There are two kinds of shells: gastropods, which are single shells, often coiled, and bivalves, which are paired and joined by a small hinge.

Seaweed is algae that lives in the sea. There are many different types. Sea belt is known as 'poor man's weather glass' because it becomes soft before rain and brittle during dry weather. When it dries out, it becomes covered with a sweet white substance which gives sea belt its third name – 'sugar wrack'.

Surfers travel the world with their boards, looking for the 'perfect wave'. Many of them head for Hawaii, in the Pacific, where the Polynesians invented surfing many centuries ago. They called it wave sliding ('he'e nalu'). The Hawaiian kings used to ride the best boards, which were known as 'olos'. They were made of lightweight wili wili wood and could be up to seven metres long. Nowadays, boards are made from foam and fibreglass – usually two metres long for very experienced surfers.

Summer Sports

Beautiful summer days, with their extra hours of daylight, are perfect for all sorts of outdoor sports – whether you are competing yourself, just joining in for fun or supporting your favourite team.

Venus Williams (above), of the United States, started playing tennis when she was four years old. She has now won two of the four top Grand Slam titles in the world – Wimbledon (UK) in 2000 and 2001, and the US Open in 2000. The other two main tournaments are held in France and Australia.

Cricket was first played in England over 300 years ago. The rules, drawn up in 1788, have survived almost unchanged to this day. Shaun Pollock (above), the captain of the South African cricket team, is considered one of the finest all-round players today.

Baseball is a direct descendant of two British games – cricket and rounders. Although baseball is played in over 120 countries around the world, including Japan and Australia, it is often known as the United States' 'national pastime'. The Major League baseball season lasts from early April until the first week in October.

The first official game of baseball was played between the Knickerbockers and the New York Nine in Hoboken, New Jersey, in the autumn of 1845. Twenty three years later, it became a professional game. Nowadays, there are 30 Major League baseball teams throughout the United States and Canada, divided into the National League and the American League. Each season, since 1903, the champions from each league have met in the World Series. Baseball was played for the first time as an official Olympic sport at Barcelona in 1992. At the Sydney Olympics in 2001, when professional athletes were allowed to compete, the United States defeated Cuba to win the gold medal.

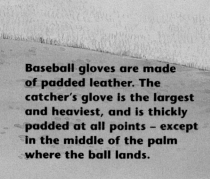

Baseball gloves are made of padded leather. The catcher's glove is the largest and heaviest, and is thickly padded at all points – except in the middle of the palm where the ball lands.

Midnight sun festival

The summer solstice is the longest day and shortest night of the year. This is usually celebrated on 21 or 22 December in the southern hemisphere and 21 or 22 June in the northern hemisphere. In countries that lie to the extreme north, such as Alaska, Finland and northern Sweden, the sun hardly sets at all at this time of year.

Midnight sun festivals are held in different parts of Alaska during the third week of June, with midnight baseball games, soccer tournaments and marathon races that need no artificial lighting. The celebrations in the town of Nome take place in the far north-west of the country, just 164 kilometres south of the Arctic Circle. At this time of year, there are 22 hours of direct sunlight on the longest day (21 or 22 June) and the sun just touches the horizon at night but does not set. The midsummer events at Nome include a festival parade and the Nome river raft race (right).

O Bon is a Japanese festival which is usually held in mid-July or August for a week. It is the time when the souls of departed ancestors are believed to return home, and has many different names, including 'Feast of the Dead'. Families clean their ancestors' graves and altars in their homes and decorate them with flowers. They also leave vegetables, fruit and rice wine for the spirits to enjoy. Bright red lanterns are hung up during the week to guide the spirits on their return. There are all sorts of different festivities, including fireworks at night.

Traditionally, midsummer has also been a time of great celebration and revelry in northern European countries as the sun reaches its height. Over the centuries, there have been all sorts of customs associated with it, mostly to do with lighting great bonfires, perhaps to represent the sun, and dancing round them or even leaping through them!

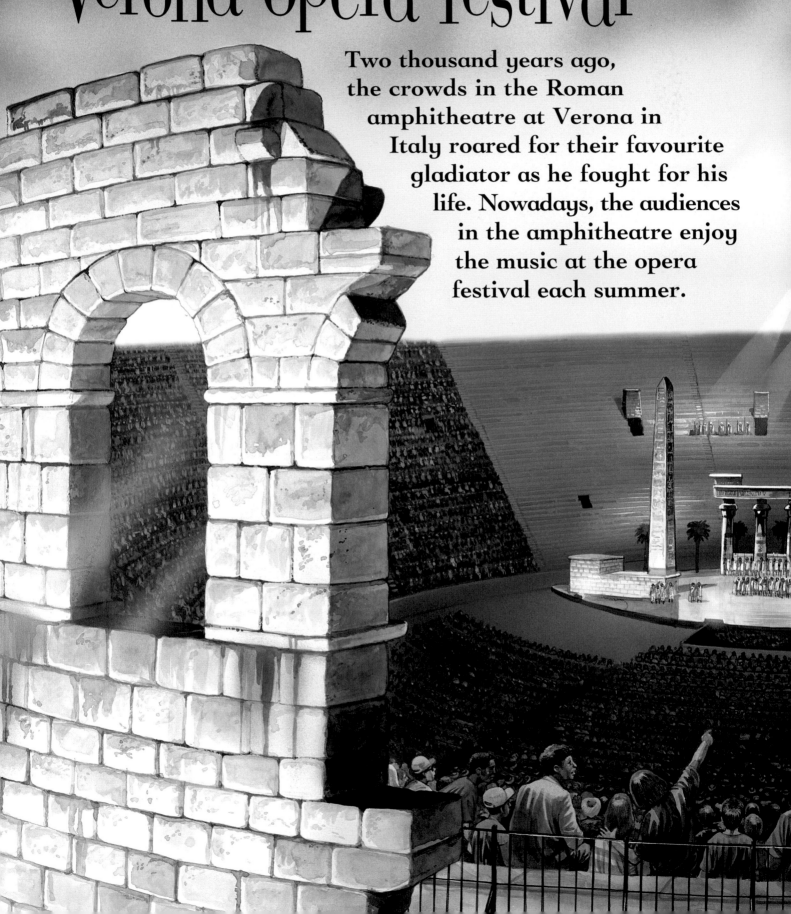

Verona opera festival

Two thousand years ago, the crowds in the Roman amphitheatre at Verona in Italy roared for their favourite gladiator as he fought for his life. Nowadays, the audiences in the amphitheatre enjoy the music at the opera festival each summer.

Every year, more than 500,000 visitors come to the historic town of Verona for the summer opera festival. It takes place each night of the season, under the stars, in the huge amphitheatre, which can hold up to 15,000 spectators at a time.

The amphitheatre was built in the first century AD during the last years of the Emperor Augustus and originally held 30,000 spectators. At the time, it was the third largest amphitheatre in the world. It is remarkably well-preserved but lost most of its outer ring in an earthquake which devastated the town in 1117. Over the years, it has been the setting for a variety of spectacular events – including bloodthirsty gladiator contests, which were so popular in Roman times, as well as jousts and tournaments. It has been the home of the opera festival since 1913 but is also a venue for ballets and jazz, rock and pop concerts.

Each night of the opera festival, members of the audience can buy a little candle when they enter the amphitheatre. As the opera begins, the lights twinkle in the dusk.

In Kandy, Sri Lanka, the summer festival of Esala Perahera is held in honour of a single tooth, which is believed to have belonged to the Buddha. It is known as the 'Relic' and is kept in a golden casket in the Dalada Maligawa – the Temple of the Tooth. On the final night of the festival, a replica of the Relic is paraded through the streets under a canopy of lights. It is carried on a elephant known as the Maligawa Tusker.

AUTUMN

Autumn marks the turning of the year as the heat of summer fades. The harvest is brought in from the fields and fruit is picked from the orchards. Animals are busy collecting food, too, and storing it for the months ahead. The leaves on the trees start to change colour and fall, swirling through the air in the blustery autumn winds.

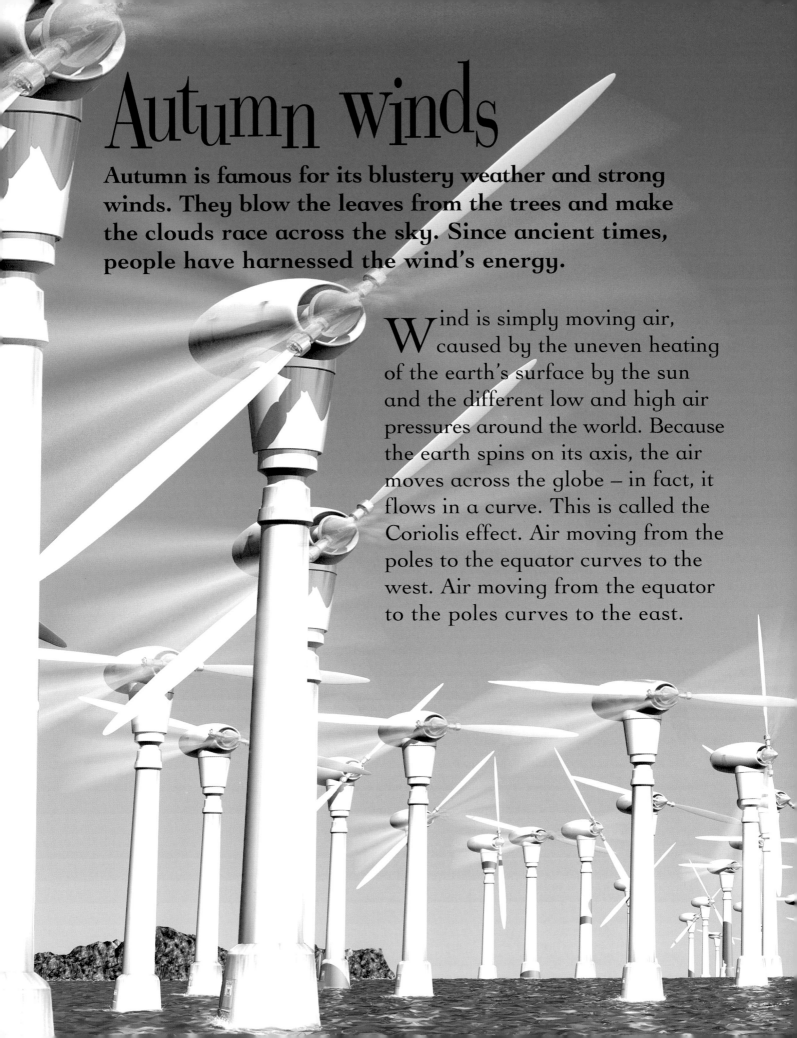

Autumn winds

Autumn is famous for its blustery weather and strong winds. They blow the leaves from the trees and make the clouds race across the sky. Since ancient times, people have harnessed the wind's energy.

Wind is simply moving air, caused by the uneven heating of the earth's surface by the sun and the different low and high air pressures around the world. Because the earth spins on its axis, the air moves across the globe – in fact, it flows in a curve. This is called the Coriolis effect. Air moving from the poles to the equator curves to the west. Air moving from the equator to the poles curves to the east.

More than 5,000 years ago, the Egyptians used the wind to sail their ships on the Nile river. The Persians used windmills to grind their wheat and other grains. Nowadays, more and more electricity is being generated on wind farms. The wind machines are sometimes as tall as 10-storey buildings. They have huge rotating blades that look like giant propellors – up to 18.3 metres wide. The machines have to be as tall and wide as possible to capture more wind.

There are two different kinds of wind machine – one with a horizontal axis, the other with a vertical axis. They can operate only when the wind is blowing 22.5 kilometres per hour or more, which occurs about 25 per cent of the time. But when the wind is blowing harder than this, extra electricity is produced and stored in special batteries.

Wind is a clean, renewable energy source. It does not use up precious natural resources and will not run out – as long as the sun goes on shining!

It is often very important to know what the wind conditions are – particularly if you are going to sail a boat or fly a plane. The direction from which the wind blows is shown by a weather vane. This usually looks like an arrow with letters to show wind direction – for example, 'E' for east. But the speed of the wind is measured by an anemometer which spins round and round. The most common type looks like a small windmill with four cups fixed to the central shaft (left). Wind speed is measured in knots for ships and aircraft, with one knot being equal to 1.85 km/h. The Beaufort Scale, invented in 1805, gives wind speed as a 'force' from 0 (calm, 0–1 km/h) to 12 (hurricane, over 119 km/h).

Autumn colours

As the heat of summer disappears, nature struggles against the chills of autumn to put on a spectacular display of colour in the woodlands. Trees turn coppery reds, while nuts, berries and toadstools spring into life, and flowers such as the purple autumn crocus bloom.

Trees that lose their leaves are deciduous. Their leaves contain a special, bright green chemical called chlorophyll, which needs sunlight to produce food for the tree from air and water. As the sun's warmth fades during autumn, leaves lose their green colour and fall to the ground, and trees start to shut down for winter.

The red maple is a stunning sight in autumn. Its leaves turn shades of orange or deep red as the shorter days cause chemical changes in the tree. Maples that turn red are usually male, whereas female maples tend to be yellowy orange in colour. Soil conditions also affect the colour of the leaves – the more acid the soil, the deeper the red.

As a species, the ginkgo biloba tree has been around for nearly 300 million years. Its distinctive, fan-shaped leaves turn yellow in autumn. Chemicals from its leaves and seeds are used to treat conditions such as memory loss and vertigo.

Aseroe rubra, which means 'disgusting red', is a strange Australian fungus that grows in autumn. Also called the starfish stinkhorn, it oozes a foul-smelling slime that attracts flies. The flies spread the fungus' spores so that it can reproduce.

Coniferous trees, such as pines and firs, do not lose their leaves in autumn. Pine trees drop scaly cones. The scales open, releasing seeds, in warm, dry weather and close in the damp and wet – so the cones can be used to forecast weather.

Autumn fauna

In the autumn, animals and birds begin to get ready for the winter ahead. They stock up on food while there is plenty around and build cosy nests and shelters to keep themselves safe and warm.

Grey squirrels enjoy all sorts of different food, according to the season, and in autumn their diet usually consists of nuts, seeds, acorns and berries.

Like many other creatures, they eat as much as possible at this time of year so that they put on weight (layers of fat) to see them through the winter. They collect extra stores, too, and bury them underground to eat later, when food is scarce. They find these secret hoards again, months later, by using their highly developed sense of smell. Occasionally, of course, the odd store will get forgotten and the nuts will germinate and sprout into a clump of new trees. Squirrels sometimes make their homes in holes or cavities in tree trunks. But they often build large nests made out of leaves and twigs near the tops of large trees. These are known as dreys and can be seen in the bare branches as winter approaches.

Many creatures that hibernate prepare their winter quarters during the autumn months. Hedgehogs make their large nests in sheltered spots where they can curl up tight for four or five months. It might be under a pile of leaves or an old compost heap or in the root of a tree.

Each autumn millions of monarch butterflies gather in southern Canada to migrate thousands of kilometres south to Central America.

The fox has a tawny coat and white tipped brush, or tail. As wintertime approaches, the fur becomes thicker to keep out the biting cold.

Jays pick acorns from oak trees. They fly off with them in their beaks and bury them in the ground. In winter they return to their hidden stores.

Badgers prepare their setts by bedding them with moist leaves which generate warmth, and blocking passages to keep out the cold and intruders.

Autumn farming

Autumn is harvest time for most countries; farms are at their busiest, and many major crops are ready to be brought in. Farmers look to the skies and hope for good weather in the coming weeks.

After long days of summer sun, the fields of corn, wheat, oats and barley are ripe. Giant machines called combine harvesters work night and day, cutting the crops and bringing in the harvest before the weather breaks.

The trees in the apple orchard are heavy with fruit, too. It is picked by hand as quickly as possible before it becomes too ripe. The apples bruise very easily, although their flesh is firm, so they have to be handled gently. Each one is placed carefully in the picking bag before being transferred into large bulk bins. The apples are washed, sorted and packed, and then some are sent off to market while others are kept in cool storage until later in the year – or used to make cider or apple juice. There are thousands of different varieties of apple, each with its own particular flavour and texture.

By the time autumn has arrived, vineyards are thick and green, and the vines are heavy with bunches of sweet, juicy grapes, which are ready to be picked. As the grapes ripen, they are checked for acidity and for sugar levels. In all the great wine regions of the world – including France, Australia, California and South Africa – the harvest (or 'vendange') is the great event of the year. In many European vineyards, grapes are still picked by hand, but machines are being used more and more.

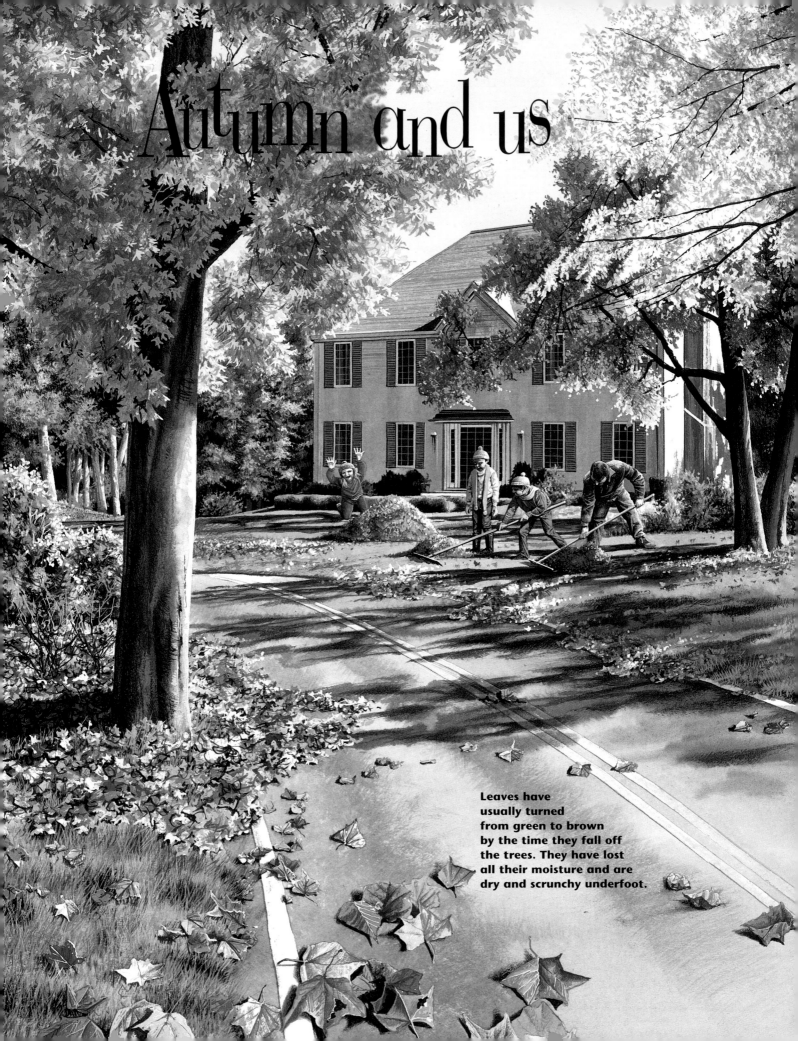

Autumn and us

Leaves have
usually turned
from green to brown
by the time they fall off
the trees. They have lost
all their moisture and are
dry and scrunchy underfoot.

Autumn is a time for raking up the leaves in the garden and lighting bonfires, for collecting conkers and picking mushrooms. Although the days are getting shorter, the weather can be lovely before winter sets in.

When a bonfire has burned right down, gardeners scatter the ash that is left – which is full of goodness – round their plants.

By mid-autumn, the leaves have fallen everywhere, covering the grass and hiding paths, filling up drains and blocking gutters. In the countryside, people sweep them up and make huge bonfires which burn slowly for days, the smoke spiralling into the air. An adult must always be there to light the bonfire, which should be made in a safe, clear and open place.

Conkers are the seeds of the horse chestnut tree. They are eaten by deer, cattle and, in the past, were sometimes ground up for sheep.

This is the conker season, when the prickly green cases that drop from horse chestnut trees open to reveal glossy brown nuts inside. A popular children's game is 'conkers', where two players attempt to smash each other's conker (the conker is threaded on a piece of string) by taking turns swinging at it. Adults play as well; each year, the World Conker Championships are held in October on the village green at Ashton, Northamptonshire, in the UK. Hundreds of contestants from all over the world take part.

Fungi, such as toadstools and mushrooms, appear in woods, fields and gardens. Some fungi are edible but always check with an adult first.

There are lots of things to do in the garden at this time of year. Plants need to be cut back and tidied up, and mulch can be made from leaves to use as fertilizer next year. Bulbs can be planted so that they will flower in spring. Birds are preparing for winter so it is a good idea to put food, such as nuts and seeds, out for them.

Native American Indians preserved blackberries by drying them. They were then mixed with dried meat to make pemmican.

67

Up in the air

Autumn days are perfect for flying kites. They soar through the air almost with a life of their own, dancing at the end of their long, thin lines.

The basic kite is a simple two-stick, which is often known as a 'diamond'. It has one line and usually has a very long tail.

Some kites are highly decorative and brightly coloured. They look like beautiful birds or insects flying through the sky.

Stunt kites have two or more control lines, with handles, so that they can be steered through the sky to perform tricks.

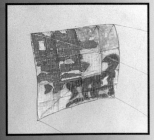

The Japanese Sagami giant kite, which is 14.4 metres square, weighs almost 880kg and needs 90 people to hoist it high into the air.

No-one is quite sure when kites were invented but they have certainly been swooping through the skies, in various forms, for more than two thousand years. Over the centuries, they have been used in various – and sometimes surprising – ways.

In New Zealand, the Maori people made kites in the shapes of birds to carry messages to the gods. Stories from ancient China describe daring exploits in times of war when soldiers were hoisted into the air on large kites to spy over enemy territory. Other tales tell of kites equipped with whistles which screamed through the night-time skies to terrify the opposing army. The Wright brothers used kites to test their theories for the first flying machine. More recently, special kites have been used to carry meteorological instruments to learn more about the planet's weather.

Kites come in all sorts of
different shapes and sizes,
and are made out of the latest,
hi-tech materials, which are
both tough and light. Diamond,
delta and dragon kites fly well
in light to medium winds, while
box kites fly better when the
winds are much stronger.

Thanksgiving

Thanksgiving, on the fourth Thursday in November, is perhaps one of the greatest celebrations of the year in the United States. Families across the continent sit down together to enjoy a traditional Thanksgiving feast.

The history of Thanksgiving, which is now a national holiday, dates back many centuries to the Pilgrim Fathers' very first harvest in 1621. They had endured terrible hardship during their first year in the New World. So, secure in the knowledge they now had enough food for winter, they sat down with their neighbouring native American Indians to give thanks.

Festivals of light, which mark the approach of winter, are found in many cultures around the world. The Hindu celebration of Divali (Deepavali) lasts for five days and takes its name from the tiny clay lamps, known as diyas, that are lit in every home after sunset. There are many traditions to be observed, such as decorating the cattle or taking ritual baths.

In 1817, New York State adopted Thanksgiving Day as an annual custom and by the middle of the 19th century many other states also celebrated a Thanksgiving Day. In 1863, President Abraham Lincoln appointed a national Day of Thanksgiving on the last Thursday in November but this was changed by President F D Roosevelt, in 1939, to the fourth Thursday in November. However, in Canada, Thanksgiving is always celebrated on the second Monday of October.

Roast turkey, cranberry sauce, sweet potatoes, corn on the cob and pumpkin pie are usually served at a typical Thanksgiving dinner. The Pilgrim Fathers, who had been shown how to catch wild turkey and grow unfamiliar crops by the native American Indians, probably enjoyed a similar meal.

Chinese moon festival

The moon festival is celebrated by Chinese communities around the world, on the 15th day of the eighth month of the Chinese year. Because this is lunar – governed by the moon – the exact date is not always the same, but it usually falls in September or October in the western calendar.

During the moon festival, people celebrate the harvest moon, which is at its brightest and fullest, and hangs like an enormous disc in the autumn sky. Traditionally they give thanks that the crops have been gathered in safely from the fields and that the hard work of harvesting is over for another year.

Hallowe'en, on the night of 31 October, used to be known as the 'night of the dead'. It was believed that ghosts returned to roam the earth – and witches and evil spirits were out in force on the eve of All Saints' Day on 1 November. Traditionally, people have always got up to mischief on Hallowe'en, but nowadays, children dress up as ghosts, witches or goblins, and go out 'trick or treating' for goodies, as soon as it gets dark. They sometimes light their way with pumpkin lanterns – swedes or turnips are also used. Children should always be accompanied by an adult when they go out trick or treating at night.

Families and friends enjoy a special feast and decorate their houses with bright lanterns – often shaped like animals. They admire the splendid moon – as long as it is a clear and cloudless night – and think about the moon goddess, Chang-O, who is said to have floated up to the moon, long ago, after drinking the elixir of everlasting life. Moon festival altars are laden with dishes of round fruits, such as apples, peaches and small melons, to symbolize the moon as well as family togetherness. Specially-made moon cakes are eaten. They are piled up in little groups (pyramids) of 13 to represent the 13 lunar months in the Chinese calendar.

WINTER

Winter brings frost and snow, and
temperatures which can drop below
freezing point. The sun is pale and low
in the sky now, and its rays have lost their
strength. Some creatures curl up and go
to sleep for the winter months, safe in
their underground burrows. Others set off
on their long migration to warmer places.

Winter chills

In winter, the pale sun stays low in the sky and its rays generate less warmth. As temperatures fall, weather conditions can change dramatically with thick falls of snow, sleet and hail.

During the winter months, the days are short and cold and the nights are long and dark. The winter solstice, on 21 or 22 December in the northern hemisphere and 21 or 22 June in the southern hemisphere, is the shortest day of the whole year.

When it is very cold, tiny droplets of water inside clouds freeze and form minute ice crystals. The crystals join up with each other, making the most delicate and intricate patterns, and turn into snowflakes. Each snowflake has at least 50 individual ice crystals in it. And, although every snowflake has six sides or six points, no two snowflakes are alike. The exact shape that the crystals make depends on the air temperature.

In the depths of winter, when the temperature drops below 0°C, ponds, lakes, streams and rivers may freeze. But the sea does not start to ice over until it is much colder (-2°C) because of its very high salt content.

The reindeer – or caribou – has a thick coat for warmth and splayed hooves for walking on snow.

Birds of prey – such as buzzards – are skilful hunters but food is scarce when snow covers the ground.

When the temperature has dropped below freezing point, dripping water forms icicles.

The tough, strong needles of pine and fir trees stand up to the harshest winter and the thickest snow.

Small birds – like the wren – are protected from the cold by their feathers, but they often go hungry.

High winds sometimes whip up blizzards when it is snowing heavily and cause deep snow drifts.

Hibernation

Some creatures, such as grey squirrels, shrews and foxes, are active throughout the winter months – as long as they can find food. Others, including bears, bats, chipmunks, snakes and mosquitoes, survive the winter by hibernating.

Hibernation is a very deep sleep that can last for days, weeks or months. It is a way of getting through the winter when food is scarce.

True hibernation can last for months. It is a state of complete inactivity when the body temperature drops to about 5°C, and the heartbeat and breathing slow down dramatically. Very little energy is used. During the autumn, the creature will have prepared for hibernation by eating extra food and storing it as body fat, to use for energy during the long winter ahead.

Ground squirrels and bats are true hibernators and sleep so deeply that they are almost impossible to wake up. But, from time to time, their body temperatures return to normal and they wake up. They are then active for a day or so before returning to their deep sleep again. When they are asleep, they are completely defenceless so it is important that they find somewhere secure to make their winter homes – hidden away from hungry predators.

Bears sleep between three and seven months a year, starting in early winter. During this time they do not eat, drink, urinate or defecate – thus they lose a quarter of their normal body weight.

The dormouse is known as the 'sleeping mouse' from the French word 'dormir' which means 'to sleep'. It can spend up to eight months each year hibernating in its shallow underground nest.

Chipmunks stock their burrows with large amounts of seeds to see them through the winter. They wake up from time to time, tuck into their food supply and then go back to sleep for a while.

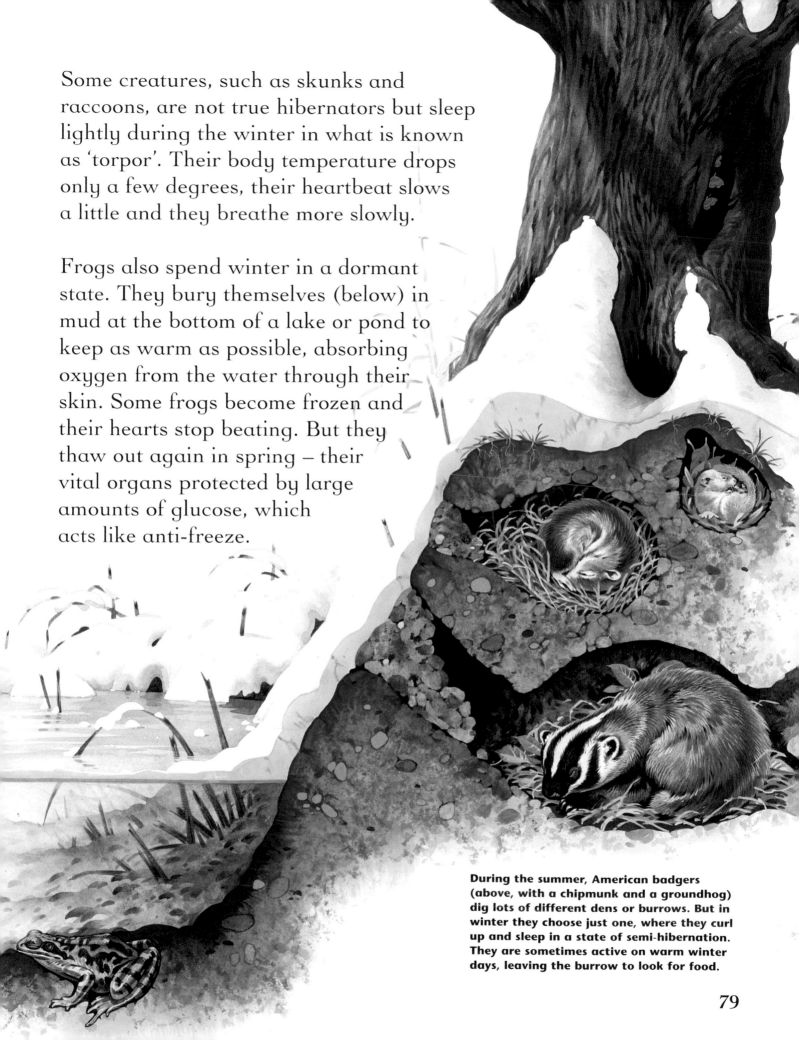

Some creatures, such as skunks and raccoons, are not true hibernators but sleep lightly during the winter in what is known as 'torpor'. Their body temperature drops only a few degrees, their heartbeat slows a little and they breathe more slowly.

Frogs also spend winter in a dormant state. They bury themselves (below) in mud at the bottom of a lake or pond to keep as warm as possible, absorbing oxygen from the water through their skin. Some frogs become frozen and their hearts stop beating. But they thaw out again in spring – their vital organs protected by large amounts of glucose, which acts like anti-freeze.

During the summer, American badgers (above, with a chipmunk and a groundhog) dig lots of different dens or burrows. But in winter they choose just one, where they curl up and sleep in a state of semi-hibernation. They are sometimes active on warm winter days, leaving the burrow to look for food.

79

Migration

Many animals, birds and fish migrate with the changing seasons. As winter approaches, some leave the cold regions, where they breed in summer, and set off on their long journey in search of warmth, shelter and food.

Each year, creatures of all shapes and sizes – including whales, butterflies, geese, caribou and wildebeest – make the journey between their summer and their winter homes. They use the same route, year after year – and generation after generation.

Some migrating animals do not travel far, perhaps just a few hundred kilometres, but others cover incredible distances. The current record is held by the Arctic tern, which travels over 16,000 kilometres from the North Pole to the South Pole and back again each year.

Birds usually migrate in large flocks. They use the stars and the sun to help them navigate – as well as major landmarks down below, like coastlines, rivers and mountain ranges. Some people think that they also use the earth's magnetic field to help them find their way. In the United States, migration is usually north-south along four major routes known as 'flyways'. In Europe, these migration routes follow a more east-west direction. But, wherever they are flying, migrating birds need the wind behind them and clear days and starry skies for a good flight.

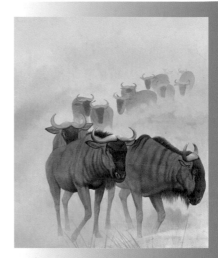

On the vast plains of East Africa, huge herds of wildebeest – or gnus – migrate nearly 3,000km each year in search of grass and water. They need to drink at least every two days and so have to live near a source of water. In the rainy season, more than 1.4 million wildebeest arrive in the grasslands of the southern Serengeti where there is plenty of food and water.

Long straggling lines – or skeins – of Brent geese fly high in the sky as they leave the Arctic and head south to the shores of the Atlantic and Pacific, where they will live on eel grass (zostera) all winter. They fly at great speed, with an occasional rest.

Wintertime

When winter arrives and the weather gets cold, it is vital to keep warm. If your temperature drops just a few degrees too low, it can be a matter of life and death.

The human body has evolved many ways of its own to try to keep warm, such as shivering. When you shiver, your muscles automatically tighten and relax very quickly indeed, burning more food for energy, and creating warmth. Your teeth often chatter at the same time, with the same result. Goosebumps appear when tiny muscles pull the fine hairs on the skin up straight, in an attempt to trap warm air.

Over the centuries, we have devised all sorts of things to keep out the chills on a cold winter's night. A heated brick or a heavy stone bottle (right), filled with hot water, were often used to warm the sheets before rubber hot water bottles and electric blankets came along. A big brass warming pan, full of red hot coals, was another solution. It had a long, wooden handle and a lid with lots of little holes to let the smoke out.

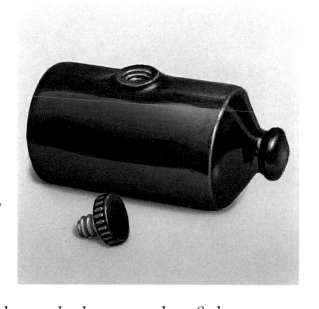

New outdoor clothes, made of the latest hi-tech fabrics, keep you warm, even when it is freezing cold. But now, new battery-heated clothes are being developed for people who have to go out in bitterly cold weather – such as mountain rescue teams or climbers. The fabric has heat-conducting metal filaments woven into it, which are connected to a small, portable battery pack.

Winter farming

Winter is one of the quietest times of year on the farm, when you cannot see very much happening. But it is just as important as any other season in the farming year.

In winter, as temperatures drop, thick frosts freeze the soil in the bare fields and help to break it up. Snow and ice accumulate deep in the earth and then melt in the spring and water the new crops. A new layer of rich topsoil slowly forms, made of dead plants and organic debris. In warmer weather, this topsoil would be devoured by insects, but in winter, they are fast asleep (hibernating) to avoid the cold.

Fresh grass is scarce so cattle are brought in to farmyards and sheds where they can be fed and kept warm and dry. Sheep, which are more hardy, often stay out all winter. If the ground is covered with snow, the farmer will take bales of hay to them in the fields.

Pineapples are grown in tropical and semi-tropical countries where it is hot all the time – they do not have a winter season. The main producers are Hawaii and Malaysia. Because there is no winter, they can grow and harvest pineapples all the year round. The plants are grown from the spiky crowns (or tops) of other pineapples that are planted in the fields – it takes about 18 months to produce the first fruit. Planting takes place through the year to make sure that there is always a good supply of pineapples, ready to be shipped off all over the world. They are picked when they are ready to eat. Like strawberries, they do not continue to ripen after they have been picked.

Winter playtime

When a blanket of fresh white snow covers the ground, the world is transformed. It does not matter where you live, in the town or in the countryside, everything looks brand new. Everyone wants to go outside to ice-skate, sledge or build huge snowmen.

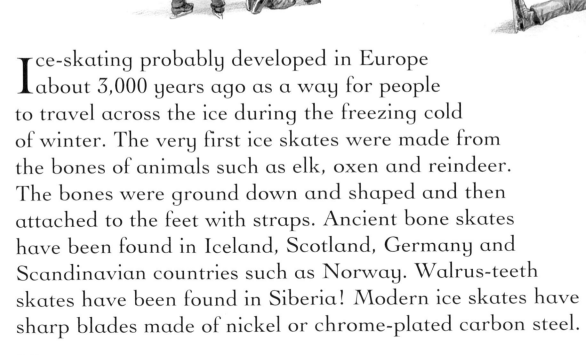

Ice-skating probably developed in Europe about 3,000 years ago as a way for people to travel across the ice during the freezing cold of winter. The very first ice skates were made from the bones of animals such as elk, oxen and reindeer. The bones were ground down and shaped and then attached to the feet with straps. Ancient bone skates have been found in Iceland, Scotland, Germany and Scandinavian countries such as Norway. Walrus-teeth skates have been found in Siberia! Modern ice skates have sharp blades made of nickel or chrome-plated carbon steel.

Today, most people ice-skate for pleasure – not because they have to. In 1876, the world's first refrigerated ice-skating rink, the Glaciarium, was opened in London. Then, three years later, the first indoor rink opened in New York, in the United States. Indoor ice rinks are cooled by the same technology that works for refrigerators. The surface of the ice is kept smooth and clean by ice-resurfacing machines.

Sledges come in all shapes and sizes and can be made of wood, metal or plastic. The fronts are often bent up and backwards to form 'hoods'. Ropes are attached so that passengers can hold on.

The traditional snowman has a bright orange carrot for a nose and two black eyes made out of pieces of coal. Ice and snow can also be used to make more complicated sculptures, such as the ones made every January at the winter carnival in Minnesota, US.

WARNING: Only skate on proper ice rinks and when accompanied by an adult. Never skate on frozen lakes, ponds or rivers – ice breaks easily. Always ask an adult for permission before you go out to sledge or to play in the snow.

Winter Sports

Skiing is one of the most thrilling of all winter sports – whether you are a beginner or an expert speeding down the mountain at nearly 100 kilometres per hour.

Downhill skiing first started in the Alps in Europe and so is often known as Alpine skiing. There are thousands of ski areas in the world – most of them in Europe, Canada, the United States, and Japan.

World Cup ski competitions are held each year in northern hemisphere countries from December to March.

Winter mountaineering can be difficult and dangerous. It is the most challenging time of year, with freezing temperatures and biting winds. Serious climbers are extremely fit and take no risks, following very specific procedures as they negotiate snow, rock and ice. They wear layers of protective clothing to keep warm – hats or balaclavas, gloves, goggles, and crampons on their boots. They carry ice axes and ropes as well. If they get into difficulty, mountain rescue teams are always at the ready.

The World Ski Championships are held every other year and the Winter Olympics take place every four years. There are five different kinds of races in Alpine competitions: the downhill, the slalom, the giant slalom, the super giant slalom and the parallel slalom. In slalom races, the competitors have to ski between a series of 'gates' made out of pairs of poles, set out in a zig-zag pattern down the course.

Snowboarding evolved from skiing, skateboarding and surfing. It began life in the United States in the 1960s.

Ski poles are made of aluminium or composite materials. They have a round, or star-shaped, piece of plastic called a basket, about 8cm from the bottom point – this prevents the pole from sinking into the snow. Ski boots consist of an outer shell made from rigid plastic and an inner boot made from foam.

Sapporo's Snow festival

Japan's biggest snow festival is held in February, at Sapporo, on the island of Hokkaido. The festival, known as Yuki Matsuri in Japan, began in 1950 and now attracts about two million people each year.

Huge sculptures of famous buildings and monuments, fantastic creatures and cartoon characters are carved out of snow and ice – all in incredible detail. Life-sized, multi-storey ice buildings are illuminated and are big enough for visitors to wander around inside. Some have been almost 15 metres high. Over the years, snow and ice replicas of many of the world's most famous landmarks have been made, including the Egyptian pyramids, St Paul's Cathedral in London, the Taj Mahal and the Great Wall of China. More than 3,000 sculptors take part – spending almost a month carving the huge constructions and often working at night. Lorries carry fresh loads of clean snow down from the mountains and bulldozers are used to gather the snow into position.

Makara Sakranti is the winter solstice in the Hindu calendar and is marked by the passing of the sun into the sign (Sakranti) of Capricorn (Makara). It takes place in the middle of winter – usually around 14 or 15 January – and there are many festivals all over India to celebrate the harvest and the coming of spring. In the south, the festival is known as Pongal. It takes its name from a special rice dish which is offered to the rain and sun gods. Pongal is also offered to the cattle, honouring them for their hard work.

In 1972, the snow festival
was held during the 11th Winter
Olympic Games in Sapporo, which
gave it tremendous publicity around
the world. As a result, the International Snow Statue
competition began in 1974 and now teams from all over
the world take part. They include groups from Hawaii and
southeast Asian countries where it never snows and their
only experience of ice sculpting is on a much smaller scale.

New Year

On New Year's Eve (31 December for many countries), people all over the world stay up until midnight to celebrate the New Year.

In Scotland, New Year is known as Hogmanay, the most important festival of the year – it draws huge crowds in cities such as Edinburgh and Glasgow. Although New Year is celebrated far and wide, some communities (for example, Hindus, Muslims and Chinese people) use different calendars so it falls at another time of the year.

There are different opinions about where the word 'Hogmanay' came from – possibly the Gaelic 'oge maidne' which means 'new morning'.

On the stroke of midnight, a huge firework display starts on the battlements of Edinburgh Castle, perched high on the hill above Princes Street.

But everybody agrees that the roots of Hogmanay reach back to the time when primitive people worshipped sun and fire in the deep midwinter. Over the years this changed and developed into the great Roman winter festival of Saturnalia, a time of riotous merrymaking.

Nowadays, there are enormous gatherings in the centres of large cities, like New York, Sydney and London, as well as in Scotland. On the stroke of midnight in Times Square, New York, a huge crystal ball is lowered, glittering with lights. In Sydney, Australia, a spectacular firework display takes place in the harbour and on the famous bridge. In London, the crowds sing 'Auld Lang Syne' in Trafalgar Square.

Hogmanay traditions include 'first footing'. On the last stroke of midnight, a dark-haired man is invited into the house. He must bring some coal (for warmth), bread (for food) and a coin (for wealth).

Groundhog Day, on 2 February, is now an important national event in the United States. The Mayor and citizens of Punxsutawney, Pennsylvania, gather to watch a groundhog called Phil emerge from his winter sleep. If it is sunny and Phil sees his own shadow, he has another six weeks' nap, but if it is cloudy, he stays out and the prediction is for fair weather.

SEASONAL EVENTS

JANUARY
New Year

FEBRUARY
Shrove Tuesday (Christian)
Chinese New Year
Ash Wednesday (Christian)
Nirvana Day (Buddhist)
Eid ul Adha (Muslim)

MARCH
Mothering Sunday
Al Hijrah (Muslim New Year)
St Patrick's Day (Christian)
Vernal equinox:
spring begins
Pesach (1st day Passover;
Jewish)
Good Friday (Christian)
British summer time begins

APRIL
Easter Monday (Christian)
Baisakhi Mela (Sikh New
Year)
Rama Maulmil (Hindu)

MAY
Whit Sunday (Christian)
Trinity Sunday (Christian)
Wesak Day (Buddhist)
Corpus Christi (Christian)

JUNE
Martyrdom of Guru Arjan
Dev Ji (Sikh)
Summer solstice:
summer begins

September

Rosh Hashanah (Jewish New Year)

Yom Kippur (Day of Atonement; Jewish)

Sukkot (1st day; Feast of Tabernacles; Jewish)

Autumnal equinox: autumn begins

October

Navaratri (1st day; Hindu)

British summer time ends

Hallowe'en

November

Diwali (1st day; Hindu)

Bonfire (Guy Fawkes) Night

Ramadan (1st day; Muslim)

Remembrance Sunday

Birthday of Guru Nanak Dev Ji (Sikh)

Martyrdom of Guru Tegh Bahadur Ji (Sikh)

Chanukkah (Jewish)

December

Eid ul Fitr (end of Ramadan; Muslim)

Bodhi Day (Rohatsu; Buddhist)

Winter solstice: winter begins

Christmas Day (Christian)

Boxing Day

New Year's Eve

INDEX

Alaska 52
Ancient Egyptians 45, 59
Ancient Romans 55
animals 10, 13, 22–23, 40–41, 62–63, 77, 78–79, 80–81
Antarctica 10
apples 64
autumn 8, 9, 56–72

baseball 50–51
birds 23, 28, 63, 67, 77, 80–81
bonfires 33, 53, 67
Buddhism 55
Bun Bang Fai 34–35

camels 10, 41
China 68, 72–73
clothes 19, 27, 83, 88
clouds 14, 19
cold 10, 76–77, 82–83
conkers 67
constellations 30–31

deserts 10
Divali (Deepavali) 70
dogs 28, 29, 41

electricity 45, 59
elephants 40–41, 55
Esala Perahera 55

farming 24, 46, 64, 84
festivals 32–35, 46, 52–55, 70–73, 90–95
flowers 18, 20–21, 22, 46, 47
frogs 23, 79
fruit 46, 64, 67, 72, 84
fungi 60, 67

gardens 67

global warming 9, 38
gods and goddesses 27, 34, 45, 72
Groundhog Day 93

Hallowe'en 72
harvest 64, 72
heat 10, 12–13, 39, 40–41, 44–45
hibernation 63, 78–79, 84
Hinduism 33, 70, 90
Hogmanay 92–93
Holi 33
Holland 20
honey bees 42–43
human body 45, 83
hurricanes 15

ice 10, 45, 77, 84
ice sculpting 90–91
ice-skating 86–87
insects 20, 22, 42, 63, 84
Inuit 34
Ireland 32–33
Italy 54–55

Japan 52, 68, 90–91

Kalahari bushmen 12
keeping cool 40–41, 45
kites 68–69

lambs 24–25
leaves 60–61, 66–67

Maori people 68
Mars 9, 30
meteor showers 31
midnight sun 52–53
migration 63, 80–81
moon festival 72–73

native Americans 46, 67

New Year 92–93
night 30–31, 52–53, 76, 83

O Bon 52
opera festival 54–55

parks 28–29
penguins 10–11
planets 9, 30
pond life 22–23

rain 18–19, 34
rainbows 19
rocket festival 34–35

St Patrick's Day 32–33
savannas 12–13
Scotland 92–93
seaside holidays 48–49
seasons, cause of 9, 38–39
skateboarding 28
skiing 88–89
snow 76–77, 84–87
snow festival 90–91
solstices 38–39, 52, 76, 90
sports 50–51, 88–89
spring 8, 9, 16–33
spring cleaning 26–27
spring equinox 27
Sri Lanka 55
summer 8, 9, 36–55
sun 9, 12, 18, 38–39, 44–45, 52–53, 60, 76
sunflowers 46–47

Thailand 34–35
Thanksgiving 70–71
Toonik Tyme 34
tornadoes 14
trees 12, 18, 20, 28, 29, 60–61, 77

USA 33, 50, 70–71, 87, 93

water 10, 12–13, 40, 41, 84
weather 6, 18–19, 68
winds 14–15, 58–59, 77
winter 9, 74–93